C000151445

# PERFECT PIES

Tamasin Day-Lewis

# PERFECT PIES

POSH PIES, EVERYDAY PIES, NEW PIES
& OLD FORGOTTEN FAVOURITES

WEIDENFELD & NICOLSON

**Tamasin Day-Lewis**, a finalist in the *Independent* Cook of the Year competition in 1994, is now widely regarded as one of the great food writers of our time. She writes an avidly followed column for Saturday's *Daily Telegraph* and is a regular contributor to American *Vogue*, *Vanity Fair* and *Country Homes and Interiors*.

After reading English at King's College, Cambridge, she went on to direct many television documentaries for the BBC, ITV and Channel 4.

Tamasin's approach to cookery celebrates comforting, rural recipes, champions seasonal dishes and rekindles the pleasures of 'proper', slow cooking. Her last six books,

*West of Ireland Summers: A Cookbook* (1997), *Simply the Best* (2001), *The Art of the Tart* (2000), *Good Tempered Food* (2002), *Tarts with Tops On* (2003) and *Tamasin's Weekend Food* (2004) have all been widely and well reviewed and she has recently completed her second 15-part television series, 'Tamasin's Weekends'.

Tamasin lives in Somerset and County Mayo in Ireland.

# CONTENTS

'Is there anyone who doesn't inwardly melt at the sight of a golden glazed pie crust with its little cottage chimney of steam wafting the scent of buried juices, the auguries of delight of what lies beneath? A classic, a soothing chicken pie, the crisp crumbliness of a raised hot water pie crust, the sugar-topped exuberance of a fruit pie, its crackling sweetness concealing the acid fruit below, the buttery spiced whiff of an apple pie…'

*Perfect Pies* is a celebration of this most traditional, comforting and delicious of foods, as enjoyable in the making as in the eating.

In this book I will show you how to make pastry for every type of pie, easy infallible recipes which produce pastry invariably superior to anything you can buy.

Savoury or sweet, homely or sophisticated, traditional or innovative, this book has a pie to impress for every occasion.

*Tamasin Day-Lewis*

'Pies are the business. You can dress them up or dress them down. Make them classic or modern, savoury or sweet, shroud them in butter-crisp pastry or top them with creamy potato. No food comforts and nurtures like a proper home-made pie.'

# RECIPES

**Serves 4**

1.5kg/3¼lb organic free-range chicken and
  some extra carrots, celery, onions and herbs
2 medium carrots, sliced into thick discs
2 stalks celery, chopped
2 fat white wands of leeks, sliced into discs
  (use tops when poaching chicken)
2 medium onions, peeled and quartered
55g/2oz unsalted butter
55g/2oz flour

150ml/5fl oz full-cream milk
150ml/5fl oz chicken stock from poaching
  the bird, reduced by half by boiling
150ml/5fl oz double cream
sprigs of tarragon and flat-leaf parsley, chopped
sea salt and black pepper
shortcrust pastry made with 340g/12oz plain
  flour and either 170g/6oz unsalted butter or
  lard, or half butter and half lard (see p.36)
beaten egg for glaze

# CHICKEN PIE

Put the chicken in a tightish-fitting pot with some leek tops, carrot, celery, onion, a few peppercorns and a bouquet of fresh herbs. Cover with water, bring to the boil slowly and skim. Cover the pan and poach the chicken for 45–60 minutes, turning it over at half time. Make the pastry, then wrap it in clingfilm and put it in the fridge for half an hour.

Steam the vegetables; carrots first, celery next, then the onion and leek for the last 5 minutes. Preheat the oven to 180°C/350°F/Gas 4 and place a baking sheet on the middle shelf of the oven to heat up.

When the bird has cooled down, remove and tear the flesh, along the grain, pulling it into long bite-sized pieces.

Make a roux with the butter and flour, then add the milk and chicken stock, both hot, alternately, until you have a satin-thick sauce, then add the cream. Remove from the heat, season and add two tablespoons of chopped fresh herbs. Stir in the chicken and vegetables and leave to cool.

Line your buttered pie dish with two-thirds of the rolled-out pastry, then evenly spread out the filling. Cover with the remaining third of the pastry, and crimp the edges. Brush the top with beaten egg. Cut a cross in the middle of the pie to allow the steam to escape as the pie cooks. Bake for about an hour, then check. If the pastry is beautifully bronzed, cover the top with a sheet of greaseproof paper and cook for about another 15 minutes. Don't cut into the pie for at least 10 minutes after taking it out of the oven.

**Serves 6**

900g/2lb boned shoulder of pork, half minced and half cut into 1cm/½in dice; you need the high fat content of shoulder

225g/8oz thin unsmoked green back bacon, again, half minced, half chopped small (speak sweetly to your butcher)

2–3 tsp fresh sage, finely chopped

½ tsp each cinnamon, nutmeg and allspice; grind the spice yourself, the flavour is so much better

1 tsp anchovy essence

sea salt, black pepper

hot water crust pastry and jellied stock (see p.38)

# MELTON MOWBRAY PORK PIE

Put all the meats into a large bowl, add all the seasonings and mix well together by hand. Pack the filling tightly into the pie or pies, then roll out the lid and put it on top with the help of some beaten egg. Cut a central hole, through which the steam can escape, and decorate with pastry trimmings as you will. Brush egg all over the pie and start the cooking at 200°C/400°F/Gas 6 for the first 30 minutes. Reduce the temperature to 170°C/325°F/Gas 3 and cook for a further hour for small pies, or 2 hours for large ones. Cover the top with greaseproof paper if it is darkening too much.

Remove the pie from the oven and take it out of its mould or paper. Brush the sides with beaten egg once more and return to the oven for 10 minutes for a little colour enhancement. Then pour the jellied stock through the hole with a small funnel; the meat will have shrunk considerably. Abandon the pie for at least 24 hours before you tuck in, but longer won't hurt. The beauty of hot water crust pastry is that it absorbs the meat juices and fat on the inside while managing to stay crisp on the outside. Serve with good home-made chutney, a slice of mature Cheddar, a celery salad – I leave it to you.

serves **6–8**

450g/1lb green back bacon rashers, the rinds
  snipped off
450g/1lb white of leek, finely chopped
225g/8oz spinach, finely chopped
1 bunch of watercress, finely chopped
a handful of flat-leaf parsley, finely chopped

2 eggs
4 tbsp Jersey double cream
120ml/4fl oz good jellied chicken stock, cold
sea salt and black pepper
shortcrust pastry made with 170g/6oz flour
  and 85g/3oz unsalted butter (see p.36)
beaten egg for glaze

# GREEN HERB AND BACON PIE

Preheat the oven to 180°C/350°F/Gas 4. Line a 1.5-litre/3-pint pie
dish with half the rashers and top with the leeks mixed with the spinach,
watercress and parsley. Beat the two eggs with the cream and pour them
over the vegetable and herb mixture, season, then add the jellied stock.
Lay the remaining rashers over the top and shroud in pastry in the usual
way. Brush with beaten egg and bake until the pie is golden brown, about
an hour.

serves 6

1kg/2¼lb cod or unsmoked haddock,
  skinned and filleted
225g/8oz or so natural smoked haddock
8 or 9 scallops with large commas of coral,
  cleaned and the white discs sliced in two,
  the corals left whole or sliced if large
  enough
290–425ml/10–15fl oz milk
55g/2oz unsalted butter

30g/1oz plain flour
1 bay leaf, nutmeg
a large glass of white wine, or better still
  vermouth
the white part of three leeks, cleaned and
  cut into rings
1kg/2¼lb potatoes, peeled, cooked
  and mashed with butter and milk
a handful of fresh dill, chopped
sea salt and black pepper

# COD, SMOKED HADDOCK
## AND SCALLOP PIE

Put the unsmoked piece of fish in a gratin dish, pour over the milk and
cook in the oven for 15 minutes. It may not be cooked right through
when you remove it, but that doesn't matter. Remove any bones and
flake the fish in large chunks into the gratin dish you're going to cook it
in, reserving the poaching milk. Meanwhile, cover the smoked haddock
in boiling water for 10 minutes. Drain the water off and flake the haddock into the gratin dish. Make a roux with the butter and flour, then
add the hot poaching milk, bay leaf and a suspicion of grated nutmeg and
whisk into a smooth sauce. Add the wine or vermouth, cooking it down
for at least 10 minutes. Season well with black pepper, but go easy on the
salt as smoked fish carries a lot of it. Steam the leeks until tender and add
them to the fish.

Preheat the oven to 180°C/350°F/Gas 4. Put the raw scallops and the
coral in with the fish, then strew the handful of dill into the sauce and
pour it over the fish. Cover with mashed potato, ruffle the top with a
fork and dot with butter. Place on a baking tray and consign to the heat
for about 30 minutes. The sauce often erupts through the potato like a
geyser and courses down the sides, which is part of the charm of the finished offering. One of the few dishes that really should be brought to the
table nuclear hot.

Serves 6–8

1.2kg/2½lb leeks, washed thoroughly, green parts cut away and white parts cut into very thin discs
6 large organic eggs
140g/5oz carnaroli rice
290ml/10fl oz extra virgin olive oil

9 tbsp Parmesan cheese, freshly grated
zest from 1 organic lemon and the juice of half
a bunch of fresh basil, stripped from its stalks and torn into smallish pieces.
sea salt and freshly ground black pepper
225–255g/8–9oz filo pastry

# LA TORTA DI PORRI

Lightly beat the eggs and place in a bowl with the leeks, rice, 200ml/7fl oz of the oil, two teaspoons of salt, plenty of black pepper and the Parmesan. Add the grated lemon zest and juice. Add the basil, then mix everything together with your hands. Set the bowl aside for 3–4 hours, mixing everything around every so often to keep it lubricated.

Preheat the oven to 180°C/350°F/Gas 4. Oil a 25cm/10in springform tin, then pour the rest of the oil into a small bowl. Carefully unfold the filo pastry and remove one leaf at a time, keeping the rest under a damp tea towel so it doesn't dry out. Lay one leaf over the tin and work it down into the bottom to the base, allowing the extra to hang over one side. Brush it gently all over with a little olive oil. Lay the next leaf of filo just overlapping the first, and covering a further bit of the tin, and oil in the same way. Do the same with another two leaves of filo, then tip the filling into the tin and spread it out to flatten the top. Fold the overhanging pieces of filo over the mixture into the middle of the tin and brush with oil. If you don't have enough, add another four leaves to cover brushed in the same way. Cut them with scissors to fit inside the tin and fold the overlap over so that it makes a little ridge around the outside of the tin. Bake for 45–50 minutes on a preheated baking tray. Let the pie cool out of the oven for 10 minutes, then remove the tin and turn the torta upside down on to the baking tray, putting it back into the oven for a further 5–10 minutes to crisp up. Cool until it is just warm before eating.

**Serves 6**

285g/10oz good, strong Cheddar, coarsely
  grated
30g/1oz unsalted butter
1 large onion, peeled and chopped finely
110g/4oz potatoes, peeled, steamed and diced
2 large eggs
4 tbsp double cream

a sprig of thyme or a bunch of flat-leaf parsley,
  chopped
pinch of cayenne pepper
sea salt and black pepper
shortcrust pastry made with 340g/12oz flour
  and 170g/6oz unsalted butter (see p.36)
beaten egg for glaze

# CHEDDAR CHEESE
## AND ONION PIE

Preheat the oven to 220°C/425°F/Gas 7. Divide the pastry into two
balls, keeping one a little larger than the other. Melt the butter in a pan
and gently fry the onion until softened and translucent, then leave to
cool. Throw the onions into a bowl with the grated cheese, potato, eggs,
cream, thyme or parsley and the seasoning, and mix thoroughly with
your fingers.

  Roll out the larger ball of pastry and line a shallow greased 23cm/9in
tart tin. Tip the cheese and onion mixture into the pastry shell. Moisten
the edges of the pastry and cover with the rolled-out top piece, crimping
the edges together carefully. Brush beaten egg over the top and bake in
the oven for 30 minutes until crisp and golden brown. You can sweat
leeks instead of onions, or add buttered apple slices instead of the potato.

**Serves 6–8**

10 large eating apples, I prefer the tartness
  of Cox's to the Golden Delicious the
  Americans like
a little light brown muscovado sugar
142ml/5fl oz carton soured cream

TOPPING:
110g/4oz sugar, half light muscovado and
  half molasses
110g/4oz unsalted butter
a large tbsp golden syrup
55g/2oz flour
85g/3oz walnuts, bashed into small bits
shortcrust pastry made with 225g/8oz flour
  and 110g/4oz unsalted butter (see p.36)

# SOUR CREAM APPLE
## AND WALNUT PIE

Preheat the oven to 200°C/400°F/Gas 6. Grease a pie dish with butter,
then line it with two-thirds of the rolled-out shortcrust pastry. Let the
overhang hang loose for the moment.

Peel, core and thinly slice the apples. Toss them into a bowl with a
small scattering of sugar and the soured cream, then mix with your hands
until everything is well amalgamated. Pile this mixture into the pastry
base, packing it tightly and mounding it up towards the centre.

For the topping, process the sugars, small bits of cold butter, syrup and
flour together. Add the walnuts when you have stopped the processing
and stir them in. Take lumps of the mixture on the palm of one hand and
flatten them out with the other palm, so you have a flattened layer rather
than a crumble top, and cover the surface of the apples bit by bit. Join
the topping to the pastry edge before you cut off the pastry overhang.

Cook for 20 minutes before turning the temperature down to
180°C/350°F/Gas 4 and cooking for another 30–40 minutes. Check
that the top layer is not darkening too much and if it is, cover with a
layer of greaseproof or foil and continue cooking. The pie will smell
ready when it is ready. I am of the firm belief that apple pie is best when
left to cool for at least 3 hours after cooking, so if you want it warm or
hot, work out your cooking times accordingly and reheat very gently.

Serves 6
750g/1lb 10oz cherries,
    pre-stoned weight
1–2 tbsp Kirsch
2 dsrtsp cornflour

110g/4oz unrefined sugar
1 tbsp demerara sugar
shortcrust pastry made with 285g/10oz flour
    and 140g/5oz unsalted butter (see p.36)
beaten egg for glaze

# SUGAR-TOPPED CHERRY PIE

Stone the cherries, then macerate them in a large bowl with the Kirsch and sugar for an hour or so. Pour off the juice that has collected into a smaller bowl and stir in the sifted cornflour to thicken it. Return the thickened juice to the cherries.

Preheat the oven to 200°C/400°F/Gas 6. Divide the pastry into roughly two-thirds and one-third. Roll out the larger piece for the base of the pie and drop it into a greased pie dish. Pour in the cherry mixture. Roll out the second piece of pastry and place it over the cherries, crimping the edges together well with the tines of a fork. Brush the top with beaten egg, then throw on the demerara. Make a couple of slashes in the crust for the steam to escape through and bake the pie for about 40 minutes, or until the top has browned. Serve warm or at room temperature with clotted cream, or à la mode with home-made vanilla ice cream.

Serves 6–8

CHOCOLATE CRUMB CRUST:
110g/4oz plain flour
3 tsp Green and Black's organic cocoa powder
1 heaped dsrtsp unrefined icing sugar
55g/2oz unsalted cold butter cut into small pieces
1 egg yolk and 1 egg white

CHOCOLATE PASTRY CREAM:
4 egg yolks
4 tbsp unrefined sugar
4 tsp cornflour
500ml/18fl oz milk, scalded
1 tbsp dark rum
1 vanilla pod, split
55g/2oz best bitter chocolate, broken into small pieces

MERINGUE CHIFFON TOPPING:
1½ tsp gelatine
100ml/3½ fl oz double cream, whipped
2 tbsp dark rum
1 tsp vanilla extract
3 egg whites
6 tbsp unrefined icing sugar
½ tsp cream of tartar

# BLACK BOTTOM CREAM PIE

Sift the flour, cocoa and sugar into the bowl of a food processor, add the butter and whizz briefly. Add the egg yolk and a tablespoon or two of ice-cold water, process again until the point at which the pastry coheres. Wrap in clingfilm and refrigerate for an hour. Preheat the oven to 200°C/400°F/Gas 6. Roll out the pastry on some flour sifted with a little cocoa powder and line the greased tart tin. Bake the crust blind for 20 minutes (see p.36). Remove the beans, prick the base with a fork and brush with egg white. Return to the oven for 5 minutes.

For the cream, whisk the egg yolks and sugar together, then sift in the cornflour and blend until smooth. Whisk in the hot milk, return the mixture to the pan and stir it over a gentle heat until thickened. Add the rum, the vanilla pod seeds and the broken chocolate, stir until smooth. Add to the cooled pastry case.

For the topping, dissolve the gelatine in 2 tablespoons of water. Add it to 1cm/½ in of simmering water in a small saucepan and dissolve fully over a gentle heat. Stir this into the whipped, but not stiff, cream and blend together. Add the rum and vanilla extract, then cool briefly in the deep freeze until the mixture has thickened but is not freezing. Whisk the egg whites until stiff, add one-third of the sugar and whisk again. Add another third of the sugar and the cream of tartar and whisk until glossy. Fold the remaining sugar in gently with a metal spoon, then fold the meringue into the gelatine mixture and dollop it on to the tart. Refrigerate for at least a couple of hours. Decorate with grated chocolate or sifted cocoa powder.

**Serves 6–8**

COOKIE-CRUMB BASE:
225g/8oz chocolate cookies, plain not covered in chocolate
1 tbsp Green and Black's organic cocoa powder
110g/4oz unsalted butter, melted

FILLING:
1 vanilla pod
570ml/1 pint Jersey milk
6 egg yolks
110g/4oz unrefined caster sugar
2 tsp cornflour
290ml/10fl oz double cream

RASPBERRY SAUCE:
225g/8oz fresh or frozen raspberries (you can double these quantities and the sugar below if you like lashings of sauce)
55g/2oz unrefined caster sugar
a little lemon juice

# RASPBERRY RIPPLE
## ICE CREAM PIE

To make the crust, put the cookies and cocoa powder in a food processor and blitz to crumbs. Add the melted butter and process again to combine. Take a deep 23cm/9in tart tin with a removable base, line with cookie-crust mixture and refrigerate.

Remove the vanilla pod seeds and place them with the pod and the milk in a saucepan. Bring to the boil, remove from the heat, cover and leave the milk to infuse for 30 minutes. Remove the vanilla pod.

In a separate bowl, beat together the egg yolks, sugar and cornflour. Pour the milk over them, whisking as you go, and return to the pan. Cook over a low heat for up to 10 minutes, whisking, until thick. Pour into a bowl and set aside to cool in the freezer. Whisk the cream and fold it into the cold custard, then transfer the mixture to the freezer for 30 minutes.

Blitz the raspberries in a food processor, sieve them into a bowl and add sugar to taste. Stir until the sugar has dissolved. Add a squeeze of lemon to bring out the flavour.

Scrape the ice cream into the cookie crust, then, with a dessertspoon, cut down into the ice cream with spoons of the raspberry sauce so that it penetrates as far down as possible. Keep the rest of the sauce to pour over later. Freeze overnight. Transfer to the fridge for 30 minutes before you want to eat it, then ease the tin away and serve with a jug of raspberry sauce.

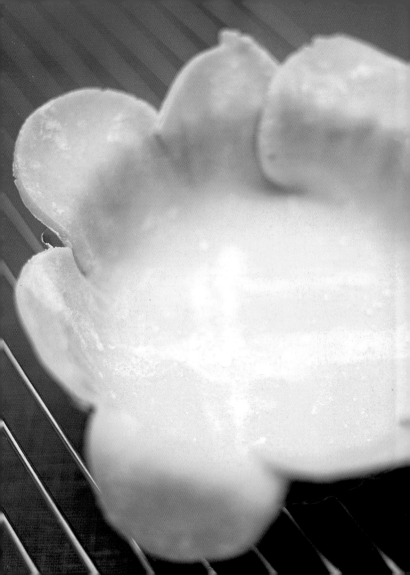

# MAKING PASTRY

*The golden rule for pastry is cold, cold, cold. Your butter should be chilled, your hands cold and you need a cold slab to roll the pastry out on. If you use a food processor, stop the button the minute the flour and butter have cohered into a ball. Warmth and overworking are the enemies of good pastry.*

# SHORTCRUST PASTRY

Use twice the weight of plain flour (preferably organic) to unsalted butter — see individual recipes for quantities. Some recipes call for half butter, half lard.

Sift the flour and a pinch of sea salt into a food processor, then cut the
cold butter into small pieces on top of it. I process it for 20–30 seconds,
then add ice-cold water through the top, a tablespoon at a time — 2–2½
should do it — with the machine running. If the paste is still in crumbly
little bits after a minute or two, add a tablespoon more water, but
remember, the more water you use, the more the pastry will shrink if you
bake it blind. One solution is to use a bit of cream or egg yolk instead of
water. The moment the dough has cohered into a single ball, stop, remove
it, wrap it in clingfilm and put it in the fridge for at least 30 minutes.

If you're making pastry by hand, sift the flour into a large bowl with
the salt, add the chopped butter and work as briskly as you can to rub
the fat into the flour. Use the tips of your fingers only, rather like running grains of hot sand through your fingers. Add the water bit by bit as
above; wrap and chill the pastry.

If you're making a double-crust pie, divide the pastry into roughly
two-thirds and one-third. Then scatter a bit of flour on your work surface, roll your rolling pin in it, dust the palms of your hands, and start
rolling. Always roll away from yourself, tuning the pastry as you go, and
keep the rolling pin and work surface floured to prevent sticking.

# BAKING BLIND

If you're baking your pastry case blind, preheat the oven to
190–200°C/375–400°F/Gas 5–6. Line your greased pie tin with pastry.
Never stretch it, it will stretch back. Try to leave at least 30 minutes for
the unbaked pastry to commune with the inside of your fridge. Or put it
in the night before you need it.

Tear off a piece of greaseproof paper a little larger than the tart tin and place it over the pastry. Cover the paper with a layer of dried beans; the idea is to prevent the pastry from rising up in the oven. When the pastry is nearly cooked (the timing depends on the rest of the recipe), remove the paper and beans and prick the base of the pastry to let out trapped air that would otherwise bubble up. Return the tart to the oven for 5–10 minutes to dry the pastry base. Brushing the partly baked pastry case with a light coating of beaten egg or egg white ensures a crisp finished tart.

# PUFF PASTRY*

Sift the flour and salt into a mixing bowl, then rub in 25g/1oz of the butter, as for shortcrust pastry, or use a food processor. Mix in the water and then gently knead the dough on a floured surface, preferably marble. Wrap it in clingfilm and refrigerate for 30 minutes.

Keep the rest of the butter out so that it softens, then flatten it into a rectangle 2.5cm/1in thick. On a lightly floured surface, roll out the dough into a rectangle three times the length and 2.5cm/1in wider than the rectangle of butter. Place the butter in the centre of the pastry and then fold over the top and bottom of the pastry to cover the butter.

With the rolling pin, press down on the edges to seal in the butter, then give the dough a quarter turn clockwise. Now roll the dough out so that it returns to its original length. Fold over the ends again, press them together with the rolling pin, and give a further quarter-turn clockwise. Repeat the process once more, then rest the dough in the fridge for at least 30 minutes, remembering which way it is facing.

Repeat the rolling and turning process twice more, then refrigerate for a final 30 minutes before using or freezing. If the pastry gets warm and buttery at any stage during the process, put it in the fridge to chill.

* 170g/6oz plain flour, a pinch of salt, 170g/6oz unsalted butter, 150ml/5fl oz cold water

**Serves 6**

Hot water crust:
200g/7oz water
170g/6oz lard
450g/1lb plain flour
1/2 tsp sea salt
1 egg (optional)
beaten egg for glaze

JELLIED STOCK:
bones from the meat used to
  make the filling
2 split pig's trotters or a
  knuckle of veal
2 carrots, chopped
2 stalks of celery, chopped
2 onions, halved but still in
  their skins

a dozen peppercorns
a bouquet of fresh herbs
water to cover

# RAISED PIES

And before you look away and think 'it's not something I would ever do', at least read these words of cajolery! Let me tell you that buying a hinged mould will be more trouble than pulling and easing the warm paste like a stocking up the insides of a tin, and that this is, truthfully, the easiest kind of pastry you could ever hope to make. And that the simple elegance of the simply accomplished pie will startle you, your children, your guests, but possibly only you will know how easy this apparently complex dish really is. Whether you tell or not depends on how honest you are when people gasp and say how amazing you are, how they could never find the time.

To make the crust, bring the water and lard to the boil in a small pan. Tip them into the middle of the flour and salt in a large bowl and swiftly work together with a wooden spoon. You can also do this in a food processor. Add the egg for colour and richness if you like, but it is not essential. Leave the dough until it has cooled to the stage at which you can handle it, but not so long that it is actually cool. Break off a quarter for the lid and put the rest into the base of a hinged pie mould, or a cake tin if you don't have a mould. Push the pastry up the sides with your hands as quickly as you can, sealing any cracks. If the paste collapses as you are working, never fear, it just means it is a little too hot, so squidge it back into a ball, wait and start again. You can shape small pies around jam jars, but you have to be really careful prising the jars out so the pastry stands proud on its own. It is not impossible, I have done it, and manual dexterity isn't my middle name. If you are going to use this method, I would place a strip of brown paper around the pastry and tie string around the circumference so that the pies keep their shape during the cooking. I forgot to do this once and, although it didn't alter the flavour a jot, I ended up with a series of little leaning towers listing heavily to starboard or slouching dangerously to port.

To make the jellied stock, put all the ingredients into a large pan, bring to the boil, skim, then simmer for 3 hours. Strain and boil down the stock until you have about 425ml/15fl oz. It will set to a solid jelly when it cools and is incomparably better than adding gelatine to your stock, but if needs must, go ahead.

This edition first published in the United Kingdom in 2005
by Weidenfeld & Nicolson, a division of the Orion Publishing Group.
Recipes taken from *Tarts with Tops On* first published in the
United Kingdom in 2003 by Weidenfeld & Nicolson

A CIP catalogue record for this book is available from the British Library

ISBN 0-297-84411-3

Printed and bound in Italy

Weidenfeld & Nicolson
The Orion Publishing Group
Wellington House
125 Strand
London WC2R 0BB

Also available by Tamasin Day-Lewis:

*West of Ireland Summers* PB (1-841-88215-1)
*The Art of the Tart* HB (0-304-35439-2) PB (1-841-88132-5) mini HB (0-297-84359-1)
*Simply the Best* HB (0-304-35654-9) PB (1-841-88202-X)
*Good Tempered Food* PB (1-841-88228-3)
*Tarts with Tops On* HB (0-297-84327-3) mini HB (0-297-84376-1)
*Tamasin's Weekend Food* HB (0-297-84364-8) mini HB (0-297-84393-1)
*Tamasin's Kitchen Bible* HB (0-297-84363-X)